MINDSET MASTERY

MINDSET MASTERY

JUDE HAWTHORNE

CONTENTS

1 Introduction to Mindset Mastery   1
2 The Science Behind Mindset   5
3 Strategies for Overcoming Limiting Beliefs   9
4 Goal Setting and Achievement   13
5 Mindset Mastery in Practice   15
6 Conclusion and Future Applications   19

Copyright © 2024 by Jude Hawthorne
All rights reserved. No part of this book may be reproduced in any manner whatsoever without written permission except in the case of brief quotations embodied in critical articles and reviews.
First Printing, 2024

CHAPTER 1

Introduction to Mindset Mastery

Everyone has a mental and emotional foundation that determines how they experience life and the success they achieve. The process of manifesting a perfect life is by design, and this foundation comes from your mindset. The word "peace" is used as a model for the framework of your mindset. By facing fears, embracing and nourishing thoughts and feelings, you change your mindset. Neglecting fears, attaching to thoughts and feelings, and distancing from fears contribute to your mindset remaining the same. By changing your mindset, the way you see yourself and the world transforms because you are created from where you think. Instead of being in survival mode, you survive by being the best.

The number one thing to consider in cultivating a positive mindset is your neural landscape, also known as your cognitive blueprint. Your neural landscape is imprinted with fears experienced when in a core or memory-driven state. Your thinking was molded from repetitive thought patterns. Thoughts repeated multiple times get seared into the area of your brain that can turn thoughts into reality. If you repeat a thought often enough, it becomes a belief. Beliefs are how we filter sensory input. When in different states, different beliefs take over. The BS of our belief systems. There are two states of mind we need to recognize: core-state and the numerous memory-based, information-driven states. Improving your mindset begins with breaking down your belief system. Once done, you will find new, healthier beliefs.

Understanding the Power of Mindset

How do we create a certain mindset, especially about an ability or area of our lives that has caused us to feel upset or frustrated in the past? We make a decision that affects our thinking from that point forward. This can range from small but powerful resolutions, such as "I will give this a try and see what happens," to huge and life-changing decisions like "I will no longer tolerate how my behavior drags me down. I will act upon my decision of being a writer for the rest of my life." Once we make that decision, we change one tiny behavior (even if it's only a thought) as we bring together the attitude, mindset, and goals that let us act upon our decision. Our belief in our capabilities becomes our truth.

Our mindset plays a huge role in how we approach our goals (if we approach them at all), whether we give up, and how we take our successes and our failures. Mindset is the collection of thoughts and beliefs on a subject. We have a mindset about ourselves, our abilities, our possibilities, and our lives. Our writing mindset is our thoughts on writing, including our writing goals, our writing abilities, and the stories we want to share. And, just like those other mindsets, it is a mindset we can direct and change when we want.

Identifying Limiting Beliefs

The first part of the formula is actually the more difficult one in most cases. The presence of many conflicting limiting beliefs could make it harder to make changes. If by some chance, they do not recognize their existence, then the issue becomes even stickier. An obvious way to deal with this problem is to find a limiting belief and change it into an empowering belief. It means changing or modifying a belief that limits you into one that empowers you.

In the most basic terms, here are the elements of a belief change: 1. Remove or neutralize conflicting beliefs that were previously in control. 2. Install or reinforce new beliefs that would be beneficial to your progress.

When we succeeded in identifying your limiting belief, it is equally important to uncover its origins because it would be difficult, if not impossible, to remove it if you are not sure of its source. We can be influenced by many other factors than our parents, but they are the people who clearly have the greatest overall influence on us. Advertising, consumerism, societal viewpoints, and peer pressure exert a subconscious influence on us as well.

Let's get started by identifying your limiting beliefs. Try to remember the last time you had a strong desire to do something and did not take any action. Could you use the powerful motivational tools that are lying within you? Chances are, a limiting belief stopped you from making progress. You may not be able to recall the event off the top of your head right now, but take a few moments to think about it and take note of the answer once it comes to you.

CHAPTER 2

The Science Behind Mindset

The objectives of this chapter are to establish the framework of the manner in which people with very different kinds of mindsets, physical or organizational, process information and reach conclusions, and illustrate these with numerous product architecture and related examples. The examples are interesting business applications of the concepts. In Chapter 1, we discussed how artistic master designers think differently during the creation of their ultimate projects, what we called their extreme introversion mode. In contrast, we discussed how common business organizations behave (extroverted mindset) during the daily design and production of the same types of architecture. In this chapter, we show new levels of detail and what the best performing master designers and businesses are doing when they are processing information and the results of their thinking. We identify principles of working which are at variance with some elements of the extroverted mindset. For example, savvy design master designers always insist on following certain paths when they think.

The previous section described the nature of two distinct mindsets: the extroverted mindset and the introverted mindset. The aim of this section is to focus on the science and the typical cognitive processes that take place when we operate in one or the other state. To begin, it is important to state that research in this area is huge, with a lot of disjointed literature from vastly disparate fields. So, when someone asks the question, "Why does this individual have an introverted mindset or why am I feeling down or unhappy?" a simple and elaborate response is very complicated. Nevertheless, simple and real-life sensory topics suggest that conventional theories cannot satisfactorily explain phenomena, and a different way of thinking is needed. GroupLayout contains a new way of thinking. It provides a vision of firms that, in its effective practical application, can lead product and design teams to work as integrated development systems, optimize product and built-in process architectures, reduce life-cycle costs, improve product features, and increase quality and reliability.

Neuroplasticity and Mindset

The brain is made up of billions of neurons, and every thought and response you forge creates a neuron connection in your brain. It is these neuron connections—particularly those that become hard-coded—which drive your habits and automatic responses. Interestingly, each and every individual arrives in the world with a completely unique brain, with the perception of absolutely nothing that we take for granted as normal adults. Each of us constructs our unique view on the world around through the process of assimilating and internalizing each person's experiences, values, language, and all that is considered normal within the culture and environment we inhabit. This concept is reflected in the maxim that everyone sees "the world not as it is, but as we are." Influence the thoughts and impressions, and you change the person. Along with the continuous development of science, many understandings and truths that are considered irrefutable are discredited. Each time a connection between neurons is stimulated, it becomes reinforced as it activates more frequently and also more automatically.

Although everyone's upbringing, nurturing, culture, and life experiences have shaped their mind, it is important to consider your brain as a skill and a muscle that can be developed. We have already taken the time to look into the power of the subconscious, and hopefully you have recognized the way it is programmed to form the particular internal perception that becomes your mindset. This internal script both dictates how you respond to different life experiences and scenarios practically on autopilot without any conscious thought, and also influences the way you engage with the world you inhabit. So then, how will a different internal software influence these responses, your life experiences, and the final outcomes? How can an individual go about reprogramming their subconscious when they hear themselves thinking negative thoughts or voice negative attitudes that were planted as children? The good news is that the process actually becomes easier and faster as time passes! Researchers and neuroscientists have demonstrated that every single person's miraculous brain is able to continuously recreate and modify itself. This is called neuroplasticity.

CHAPTER 3

Strategies for Overcoming Limiting Beliefs

Remind yourself of past achievements. If you're struggling to have faith in your abilities, take a walk down memory lane. When have you stepped up to deliver excellent work in the past? What examples can you find where you were in a similar situation but still smashed it? By jotting down your main achievements, you are providing evidence to counter your limiting beliefs. After all, if you've succeeded in the past, what's to stop you from being equally successful now or in the future? It also invites your brain to focus on feelings of competence, confidence, and pride in your abilities.

In the last section, we talked about the most common limiting beliefs that we are confronted with and the effects of harboring them in our mindsets. We now learn 3 foolproof strategies for overcoming them once and for all. Get out of your mind and just do it. The best way to overcome limiting beliefs is to get out of our own heads and into the real world. Your limiting beliefs don't have to dictate the number of opportunities you're able to apply for, the roles you apply for, or even your willingness to take on challenging tasks. Choose to act as if you don't have these fears and self-doubts. Lead with your actions, not your fears.

Cognitive Restructuring Techniques

By changing how we feel about something, we can change our beliefs. This is a cognitively focused approach to coping with tension. We first work to better understand and adjust the thoughts we are currently experiencing. We then layer in mindfulness and other strategies to ensure that we proceed to function from that higher mind viewpoint. Cognitive restructuring is a step-by-step approach for evaluating and challenging common cognitive distortions that present as automatic thoughts. Over time, chronic negative thinking can work as an inner filter for our ability to solve and impact our lives positively. We tend to follow through on what we believe, and our thinking processes have a big impact on that. In psychology, the word for self-talking is cognitive restructuring. Over the years, the precedent has shown that we can learn how to improve our self-talking and our lives. Consider how many times you've been warned to get rid of self-sabotaging views and to prevent defeatist self-talking from preventing you from living your life to the fullest.

In the first chapter of Mindset Mastery, you will learn about the first phase of the Co-Active® coaching model: the context for effectiveness or, as we call it, coaching for efficiency. It's an inside-out structure. This is about having you, the leader, determine your inherent vision, worth, and identity. There is nothing wrong with your mindset. You restrict yourself as a result of cynical thinking. Colonel Grab-rat had firmly settled on his bed in a small room. His back was turned toward the beauty of the Château that faced his window. Little did it matter how magnificently planted his room was. His breaths and beliefs were the window bars that emphasized that he would never be able to leave his lifetime of captivity at the United States Military Academy. Our assumptions limit us in the same way. His window bars and the internal barriers we erect that prevent us from achieving our greatest potential in life. They keep us captive, just like Colonel Grab-rat.

CHAPTER 4

Goal Setting and Achievement

SMART Goals: Specific, Measurable, Action-Oriented, Realistic and Timebound are attributes that help define when the goal is to be reached and how the success of that goal is to be verified. These are the micro-objectives that motivate you and establish a quantifiable signature of small wins. SMART goals often provide a path to the realization of the bigger picture items.

Big Picture Goals: These intentions involve the greater outcomes you want from your work, personal improvement or lifestyle efforts. Think of these broad targets as stepping stones within your dreams or the rosy picture - your mission, purpose or reason - that you carry around in your head. These are often the items you need to know about when turning an experience or skill into a personal WIN. They are the over-the-horizon items that light your fire and capture your imagination and conviction.

Set Big Picture & SMART Goals You likely already know that goal-setting is a crucial piece of any intention-meeting strategy. In fact, it is typically these big picture items that inspire self-investment such as learning, skill-building or personal growth goals. However, accomplishments only come to fruition when you have a clear plan and major motivation. That being said, it's important to differentiate and even connect these types of goals:

When it comes to goal setting and achievement, it's crucial to recognize that our thinking can either hinder or promote our efforts. If you're experiencing gaps between where you are and where you want to be, there are probably some ideas and attitudes that are holding you back. To spring forward, you need to identify and address those mindset gaps. You also need to set goals that are motivating and leverage your strengths. Don't set yourself up for stagnation or failure by choosing objectives that don't inspire and tapping into talents that you don't enjoy or are not good at.

SMART Goals Framework

Setting goals is more effective if you use the SMART goals framework. SMART is an acronym that stands for Specific, Measurable, Achievable, Realistic, and Time-Bound. It greatly increases your chances of goal completion when you define the specifics of your goal. This helps to motivate you and increase the chances of getting where you want to be. Let's lay out these concepts so that you can get practical about achieving your goals.

In the world of wellness coaching, a common end-game for the client is often to have a healthy lifestyle. While we have momentum, it's important to have a clear target. That's where setting goals comes in. Goals give you a direction. They help you focus your energy so that you can make better use of your time. Setting goals also helps you to organize your resources and your time so that you can make the most of your life. These might sound like self-improvement clichés, but they are very much tied to the understanding of our social, physical, and mental well-being.

CHAPTER 5

Mindset Mastery in Practice

The topics of adopting a learning-oriented mindset, reconfiguring your mindset, becoming more flexible, embracing curiosity, questioning your predetermined interests, recognizing that abilities can be developed, and adopting a growth mindset are all interesting. But how, specifically, can you pursue mindset mastery? Is there a roadmap that anyone, regardless of background, can follow to help them transform their mindset and pursue a path of personal self-healing, as I call it? This book guides you through three activities at the heart of mindset change. It is divided into a three-step framework, which is a blueprint for a transformational journey to gain mastery over your mindset and reshape your life. Just remember that it is not enough to learn about mindset. You must learn how to change your mindset and adopt a growth mindset through mindset inquiry, mindset counseling, mindset coaching, or otherwise. The journey may be long and difficult, but the rewards are well worth the effort. What do you want to achieve in life? What dreams, goals, and objectives keep you on track? The road to true growth involves endless honest answers to these questions. Mindset change is essential for turning your dreams into goals you can actually achieve – and for transforming yourself into the person you have the potential to become.

Clearly, it matters whether you embrace a growth-oriented or fixed mindset. Extensive research links mindset to success. If you believe in your capacity to learn, understand, and grow, you set high expectations for yourself, and you achieve more, in part because you improve your ability over time. Students, athletes, scientists, and great leaders have all been shown to achieve more when they possess a growth mindset rather than a fixed one. Fixed belief puts a strain on your relationships with others, particularly those closest to you. That's why it's crucial to develop a growth mindset – the belief that people can change, grow, and learn. A belief in the possibility of change, for yourself and everyone else, means that we can acknowledge our faults, listen to criticism, forgive our loved ones for their missteps, help people around us become better communicators, and grow and learn over time. It also opens up new worlds of possibility for how we interact with others and how we interact with the world around us, and how we interpret what happens. Passages from Mindset Mastery: Overcome Limiting Beliefs and Achieve Your Goals by having a growth mindset.

According to my framework, adopting a growth mindset maximizes your chances of success. When in a mindset that's geared toward learning, you are more motivated about achieving your goals and more resilient when facing challenges. You embrace personal growth and take the necessary steps to create the life you want. Consider how you build a successful career in any field: You try to learn and perform at your best in order to succeed. Growth mindset is no different. Approaching your personal development with an openness of mind puts you in the best possible position to understand yourself, identify your goals, create plans to achieve those goals, develop and refine your skills, and achieve those goals. In short, a mindset geared toward learning in the personal development sphere is the ultimate tool of success. When equipped with the proper mindset, any person can aspire to learn and grow. People improve. This is the power of believing in the potential of growth – both your own growth and the growth of others.

Case Studies and Success Stories

After waking up to your limiting beliefs, the second step is to challenge them. A list of frequently used belief-challenging questions is made available in the third section of this book. With this toolkit of belief-challenging questions, you can challenge your beliefs and find out if they really are true. Just challenging the belief doesn't help in acquiring significant changes. You will need baby steps in rewiring your beliefs. Last but not least, to instill the belief and to make it your own, you'll need practice. The final new practice is the rebirth of belief. You'll master the belief and subsequently assimilate it. Wouldn't you like to be healed and reborn? We have seen you can transform limiting beliefs. We have seen you can choose your beliefs. Now, it is time for you to choose freedom: break free from your limiting beliefs and experience the true expression of life.

Would you like to learn techniques for transforming your limiting beliefs? Now let's look at some techniques for the transformation of limiting beliefs. The first is awareness, which is simply bringing your limiting beliefs from the shadows of your unconscious to the light of your conscious awareness. When you become aware of your limiting beliefs, you can begin to change them. There are three questions you can ask yourself to become more conscious of the beliefs that are within you. The first is "What do you want?" The second is "What's in your way of achieving what you want?" The third question you can ask yourself is "Why can't you act despite the fact your belief is true?"

CHAPTER 6

Conclusion and Future Applications

Creating a successful mindset involves developing emotional intelligence skills, which are critical in overcoming limiting beliefs and breaking through the barriers to success. By ridding ourselves of the mental blocks that hold us back, our ability to achieve our goals is profoundly enhanced. In conclusion, removing our limiting beliefs can improve our decision-making, uncover new opportunities, and lead us to our greatest accomplishments. The future holds the promise of developing technologies to help people identify and overcome these limiting beliefs individually or in groups, while fostering the growth mindset in organizations. These mental technologies can potentially work with great speed and power and change people's mindset in a lasting, positive way, helping them lead more effective lives and businesses. Furthermore, while this study focused on people who are trying to break through their limiting beliefs, acquiring the proper mental and emotional skills would allow people to identify what new students need to learn mental skills and strategies and help them develop further as well. With the proper classroom instruction and training, students' faulty thinking could be corrected, improving student performance in a variety of areas.

www.ingramcontent.com/pod-product-compliance
Lightning Source LLC
LaVergne TN
LVHW092103060526
838201LV00047B/1545